First published in 2001 by
New Holland Publishers (UK) Ltd
London • Cape Town • Sydney • Auckland

Garfield House
86 Edgware Road
London W2 2EA

80 McKenzie Street
Cape Town 8001
South Africa

3/2 Aquatic Drive
Frenchs Forest, NSW 2086
Australia

218 Lake Road
Northcote
Auckland
New Zealand

10 9 8 7 6 5 4 3 2 1

ISBN 1 85974 885 6

DESIGNED AND EDITED BY
Complete Editions Ltd
40 Castelnau
London SW13 9RU

DESIGNER: Blackjacks

Reproduction by Modern Age Repro, Hong Kong
Printed and bound in Singapore by Tien Wah Press Pte Ltd

Picture Credits

The publishers would like to thank the following: CEPHAS (front cover),
Herve Amiard/CEPHAS, Diana Mewes/CEPHAS, Tim Hill/CEPHAS,
Daniel Czap/CEPHAS, Chocoladefabriken Lindt & Sprüngli AG, the Robert Opie
Collection, Prestat, The Chocolate Society, Chantal Coady at Rococo Chocolates, Fortnum
& Mason, the Advertising Archives, Selfridges Retail Ltd and Charbonnel et Walker. Every
effort has been made to identify other illustrations. Any errors or omissions will be corrected
in future editions.

The publishers would also like to thank Hodder and Stoughton Ltd
for permission to reproduce a recipe from *The Ivy* by A.A.Gill.

135 Coast Tapas 9781859748855 £12

Discount   £ 99
            John   5   4 99

Cash   £4 99

16 12/01 12 26

CONTENTS

DRINK
OF THE
GODS

The early history of chocolate

"Ideas should be clear and chocolate thick."
SPANISH PROVERB

Chocolate is one of the most enjoyable and enduring gifts the Americas have given to the world at large.

Until Christopher Columbus was introduced to chocolate in 1502, on his fourth and final voyage to the Caribbean, chocolate had remained the exclusive preserve of the peoples of Central America and their gods.

Legend holds that the god Quetzalcoatl, a pre-Columbian deity represented by a plumed serpent, showed his subjects how to cultivate the cocoa tree as a source of strength and wealth, and how to prepare its fruit as a drink for the gods.

However, rivalry among the gods led to the downfall of Quetzalcoatl, who was ejected from Paradise, vowing that one day he would return.

The Maya people, whose kingdom was centred on present-day Guatemala, established a sophisticated civilization on one side of the

Atlantic at the same time as the Roman Empire was reaching its zenith on the other. The Maya were notable for building huge, pyramid-shaped structures. They also developed the concept of zero, which was unknown to Roman mathematicians, and a calendar that remained the most accurate in the world for well over 1,000 years, until the Gregorian calendar was introduced towards the end of the 16th century.

Working on the Aztec notion that a soldier could march all day with only chocolate to keep him going, in 1940 the US army commissioned Hershey, the leading American chocolate manufacturer, to develop a chocolate bar that could survive in a soldier's pocket in tropical climates, to give him something to eat when nothing else was to hand. Hershey swung into action following the American entry into the war after Pearl Harbour, producing 500,000 "D" field rations of chocolate every 24 hours.

The Maya were also the first people to grow cocoa systematically. In their world, cocoa beans were used as a form of currency, as well as for making the drink of the gods called "*xocolatl*".

Depending on the interpretation put on it, "*xocolatl*" has two meanings. One translates as "bitter water" (from "*xoco*", meaning "bitter", and "*atle*", "water"). The other is said to convey the sound "*xocolatl-xocolatl-xocolatl*" made by the beating stick used to stir and froth the chocolate drink when it was served to the gods or other privileged recipients.

The Toltec people, who followed the Maya, extended the cultivation of cocoa, as did the Aztecs, who ruled Central and Southern Mexico from the 13th to the 16th century, when their empire was conquered by Spanish invaders led by Hernàn Cortés.

Lindt chocolates – connecting people the world over.

By a quirk of fate, the Aztecs were convinced that Cortés (the eventual destroyer of their world) was the god Quetzalcoatl, returning to earth as he had promised. Cortés arrived in Mexico in 1519, where he was treated like a god and as a god was regularly given chocolate to drink. Seventeen years earlier, Columbus had also been introduced to chocolate on the Caribbean island of Guanaja.

The chocolate both explorers were given was a cold, refreshing, slightly bitter drink prepared from finely ground cocoa beans dissolved in cold water. Herbs, honey, fruit and flowers were added. Strange as its taste was to Europeans, all agreed that the drink boosted energy and was an ideal pick-me-up after a hard day – and as a prelude to an active night.

By the time Columbus encountered chocolate on his last voyage, he was fast losing favour at the Spanish court, this may have resulted in the unfavourable reaction given to chocolate when he returned home with the first samples tasted in Europe.

In 1527 Cortés brought cocoa beans back to Spain for a second time, where they met with a far more positive response and started a European passion for chocolate that has been accelerating ever since.

Chocolate meets coffee in this exotic evocation of the Araby of old.

Regular cocoa shipments from Spanish territories in the New World began the following year and chocolate, mixed in a variety of recipes, became prized for its medicinal qualities. Spanish society quickly took up the fashion of drinking chocolate and where the gods of ancient Mexico had once led, the aristocracy of Europe now followed.

In 1660 the Spanish princess Maria Theresa married Louis XIV of France. Believing, perhaps, that the way to a man's heart (even a king's) lay via his stomach, she included among her gifts to her new husband an elaborate chest packed with chocolate. Louis took up his wife's chocolate-drinking habit with enthusiasm.

Scenes from a late 19th-century cocoa estate and mills.

By the middle of the 17th century chocolate sweetmeats had taken Paris and other leading European cities by storm. Chocolate became established as a popular breakfast drink among the well-to-do.

To satisfy this escalating demand, the cultivation of cocoa was extended from around the Caribbean southwards to Venezuela and Peru; in time it would spread to other equatorial regions of the world. As many of these were under the control of other nations, notably the Dutch and the British, Spain lost the virtual monopoly on cocoa imports that it had enjoyed ever since the first beans had reached European shores.

*"Strength is the capacity to break a chocolate
bar into four pieces with your bare hands –
and then eat just one of the pieces."*

JUDITH VIORST, AMERICAN POET AND POLITICAL WRITER

Chocolate was enjoyed as a drink and used to make a range
of confectionery and cakes long before the first chocolate
bars became available, or even practical to make.

The Aztecs had often mixed maize flour with their chocolate
drinks to absorb excess cocoa butter, but it was the invention of a
machine which pressed cocoa butter out of the chocolate liquor
which heralded the first bars of solid chocolate.

There is some debate as to which of the chocolate
manufacturers in Europe made the first chocolate bar; the reality
is that several probably hit on the idea at the same time.
However, there is no question that the man who made possible
what became an explosion in chocolate consumption and
enjoyment was a Dutch chemist named Coenraad Van Houten.

The machine that he patented in 1825 was a hydraulic press,
which separated cocoa butter from cocoa mass. By removing two
thirds of the fat, Van Houten was able to produce a "cake" that

CONSUMING
PASS

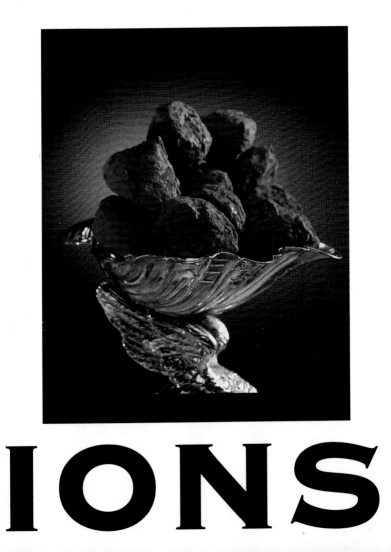

IONS

CHOCOLATS FINS

Tin advertising sign for Lindt & Sprüngli.

was considered more digestible than unpressed chocolate liquor. The resulting product became the widely popular drinking and baking food we know as cocoa.

Van Houten's chocolate presses were soon at work in other chocolate factories and in 1847 Francis Fry, whose family had for many years produced most of the commercially available chocolate in the UK, experimented with blending cocoa liquor and sugar, to which he added cocoa butter in place of water. In so doing, he created Britain's first chocolate bar.

By including cocoa butter in his blend, Fry introduced an ingredient that enabled the mixture to set in a mould. The resulting

bar may have been harsh and grainy on the palate, but it and its European counterparts, were the forerunners of every chocolate bar that has been consumed ever since.

The next milestone in the story of eating chocolate was passed in Switzerland, where the first solid bars of milk chocolate were produced in 1875, through the joint efforts of Daniel Peter and Henri Nestlé, using the evaporated milk powder which Nestlé had previously developed.

In 1892 The World's Columbus Exposition was held in Chicago, to celebrate the 400th anniversary of Columbus arriving in America. Milton Hershey, a successful caramel manufacturer from Pennsylvania, joined the crowds touring the industrial displays.

Hershey was a man quick to spot a good idea and so impressed was he by the German chocolate-making machinery he saw, that he immediately set about transforming his business – as he memorably put it, "Caramels are only a fad. Chocolate is a permanent thing."

Chocolate was certainly "a permanent thing" for the Hershey company, whose founder became known as "the Henry Ford of chocolate", through making it available to the great majority of the American population.

In addition to his business vision and success, Hershey shared similarities with several British counterparts in the chocolate business. Like the Frys, the Cadburys, the Rowntrees and the Terrys, Hershey was a Quaker.

Since George Fox had founded the Society of Friends, popularly known as the Quakers, in the middle of the 17th century, its members had been subjected to discrimination and persecution for their religious beliefs. Barred from the professions, many Quakers went into business, and among them several eminent families became manufacturers of chocolate, which they saw as a wholesome, nourishing beverage in

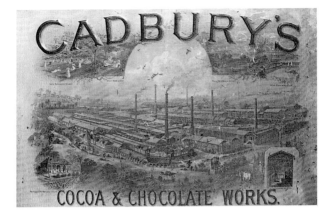

contrast to the ruinous effects of cheap alcoholic drinks, such as gin, which were having a devastating impact on the poor.

In pursuit of these humanitarian principles, successful Quaker chocolate manufacturers created working and living conditions for their employees which set a standard few employers would match for many years to come.

Bournville, close to Birmingham in central England, was created as a model village for workers past and present at the Cadbury factory around which it was built. Further north, in the city of York, the Rowntrees created a similarly agreeable environment for their employees, as Milton Hershey did for his workers at Hersheyville, Pennsylvania, U.S.A.

Together, these great pioneers widened the use and availability of chocolate, extending its tantalizing aroma and succulently satisfying taste from the boudoirs and breakfast tables of the rich, to the corner shop and market stall, where it could be enjoyed by everyone who fell under its hypnotic spell.

The heart of real chocolate

"Life is like a box of chocolates . . .
You never know what you're gonna get."
FORREST GUMP, IN THE FILM *FORREST GUMP*

Although scientists have identified some 20 species of cocoa tree, there is only one of commercial value – *Theobroma cacao*. This is the scientific name for the cocoa tree, devised by Linnaeus (Carl von Linne), the 18th-century Swedish botanist and classifier of plants. A lover of chocolate himself, Linnaeus decided that the tree from which it came merited a suitably noble name. To the Spanish word *cacao* he added *Theobroma*, which, in Greek, means "food of the gods".

Cocoa trees grow in tropical regions of high humidity, where the temperatures range from 20–30°C (68–86°F). The "cocoa belt", as it's known, extends around the globe, ten degrees north and south of the equator. The ideal plantation altitude is 400–600 m (1300–1950 ft) above sea level, where cocoa trees grow alongside taller, more robust ones, such as the banana, coconut and plantain. These help shelter the delicate cocoa trees from wind and the intense tropical sunlight: cocoa trees need at least 50 per cent shade.

A young cocoa tree starts to bear fruit – cocoa pods – three to five years after planting. Cocoa pods take up to six months to ripen. Gathering the fruit is a delicate operation. Each pod is picked by hand (a skilled picker can harvest some 1,500 pods each day)

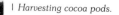
Harvesting cocoa pods.

and split open with a machete, to reveal up to 40 beans, arranged in rows of five and surrounded by a sugary white pulp.

There are three main varieties of cocoa bean. The criollo, the most exclusive and the rarest, produces chocolate of exceptional character. Increasingly scarce, it accounts for less than three per cent of the world's chocolate production.

By far the greatest proportion of chocolate (85%) comes from the forastero bean, which produces an ordinary, everyday cocoa.

The trinitario bean, which takes its name from the island of Trinidad, where it was first cultivated in the 18th century, is a hybrid of criollo and forastero beans. Like the criollo, it is a source of fine chocolate and accounts for 10–15% of world production.

Both the criollo and trinitario beans have a distinct flavour, much sought after by connoisseurs, and many of the world's leading chocolatiers take pride in producing chocolate made exclusively from one specific bean (as the accompanying picture shows).

Pure criollo (left) and pure trinitario (right) chocolate, made by Rococo, London. With 70% content of cocoa solids, Guanaja (centre) is the most exclusive chocolate, made from a careful blend of the very best beans.

FROM
TREE
TO
TRU

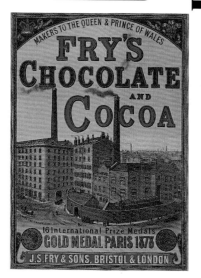

There are two main seasons for the cocoa harvest: November–January and May–July, although in very humid regions, where there is no rainy season as such, cocoa can be gathered all year round.

The first stage in preparing cocoa beans to make chocolate is known as fermentation, which can take up to a week. The cocoa beans and the pulp surrounding them are usually placed in large fermentation boxes

"Chemically speaking, chocolate really
is the world's perfect food."

MICHAEL LEVINE, AMERICAN NUTRITION RESEARCHER

FFLE

Cocoa beans drying on a plantation.

covered with banana leaves. In these, yeasts and insects get to work, breaking down the natural acidity and bitterness of the beans, and beginning the process which will develop their unique and unforgettable aroma.

The beans are regularly stirred, or moved from box to box, to let air into the whole mix and ensure a uniform fermentation.

After being removed from the fermentation boxes, cocoa beans, now brown or tan in colour, are allowed to dry. The traditional method is still practised on plantations producing the best quality cocoa. Here the beans are spread on mats or drying trays and left to dry naturally in the sun.

Once dried, the beans are stored on the plantation for only a limited period. Time is needed to examine each consignment, but when its quality has been assured, the beans need to be packed in 50 kg (110 lb) sacks, loaded into ventilated containers and shipped to the customer's port of entry.

When the beans arrive at their final destination, they are checked and sorted once again.

To reduce the moisture content in the beans further and to develop their delicate aroma, they are carefully roasted for 20 to 30 minutes. Different varieties of beans and beans from various parts of the world call for different roasting techniques; fine flavour cocoas made from criollo and trinitario beans, for instance, are roasted at lower temperatures.

When the roasting is complete, the beans are allowed to cool before being separated from their shells in a winnowing machine, which cracks the shells, breaks the beans inside into particles a few millimetres thick and removes the husks.

The remaining particles of beans, called nibs, pass to the grinding stage which transforms them into cocoa liquor, a fluid paste which is also known as cocoa mass.

Inside Lindt's Kilchberg chocolate factory in Switzerland around 1900 – from left to right one can see rollers, mills and "mélangeurs", where chocolate was blended.

The packing hall in Lindt's Kilchberg factory in Switzerland around 1900, where chocolate bars were packed by hand and sealed using sealing wax and a spirit lamp.

Cocoa liquor is the raw material from which all cocoa products are derived. Mixed with other ingredients, according to the recipes followed by particular manufacturers, it can be made into dark chocolate, milk chocolate or white chocolate.

It is from cocoa liquor that cocoa butter (cocoa's natural fat content) is also derived. Heat generated from grinding the nibs causes the cocoa butter they contain to melt. Once melted, this can either be left in the cocoa liquor or it can be removed, to be used in other production processes such as the manufacture of lipstick.

In manufacturing chocolate, further ingredients are added at the grinding stage, which gradually reduces and refines the size of the particles in the cocoa liquor.

Dark chocolate will have sugar added. Milk chocolate will have sugar and milk solids. White chocolate, which is made from cocoa

Work-rooms in Lindt's Kilchberg factory in Switzerland around 1900, where machines were only available for the heaviest work like grinding, rolling and conching.

butter alone, contains added sugar and milk solids. Many producers of premium chocolate also add pure vanilla, a tradition which dates back to the very first chocolate made in Europe, after it arrived from Central America in the 16th century.

Perhaps the most significant difference between the manufacture of high-grade chocolate and the high-volume, mass-produced, commercial product, lies in the conching process which follows grinding and mixing.

The original conching machine was a large, shell-shaped vessel (hence its name), invented by the Swiss chocolatier, Rodolfe Lindt, in 1880. Inside this, the chocolate mix is constantly agitated by paddles to create a smooth, velvety texture.

Where run-of-the-mill chocolate is conched for only a few hours, the finest quality chocolate may spend up to a week being gradually refined in a conching machine. The time allowed for this also develops the flavour of the chocolate to the full, by removing any residual acidity or unwanted aromas and dispersing the ingredients through the mixture, to produce a full, rounded, mellow aroma with the distinctive texture of top-quality chocolate.

While chocolate is conching, it is maintained at a temperature above the melting point of cocoa butter. When conching is finished, the mix must be allowed to cool carefully, so that the cocoa butter crystallizes properly and evenly throughout the blend. The technique of successive cooling and heating, which steadily reduces the temperature of the chocolate is known as tempering. Correct tempering ensures the distinctive shine and snap which are the hallmarks of premium chocolate.

The technique for moulding chocolate is the same whether it is destined for sale as chocolate bars, or as blocks of chocolate for use by confectioners to make filled chocolates, pralines and truffles. Metal moulds, held at the same temperature as the chocolate 28–30°C (82–86°F), pass along a conveyor belt to be filled mechanically with the tempered liquid chocolate. They then pass on to a vibrating belt, which settles the chocolate and removes air bubbles.

After passing through a cooling tunnel, the chocolate solidifies and is ready to be turned out for packaging and distribution.

High-capacity production line, with its newly conceived engineering and equipment controls, which went into operation at Lindt's Kilchberg factory in Switzerland in 1997.

READING
THE
WRAPPER

(The search for quality)

Jackie: "Pity there's no such thing as
Sugar Replacement Therapy."
Victoria: "There is. It's called chocolate."

VICTORIA WOOD, BRITISH COMEDIENNE AND WRITER,
FROM *MENS SANA IN THINGUMMY DOODAH*

How can we distinguish premium chocolate and the lower grade
commercial chocolate? A look at the list of ingredients printed
on the wrapper is a good indicator.

A moderate amount of sugar enhances quality chocolate,
balancing its natural bitterness and developing its flavour. Set against
this judicious use of sugar is the large amount found in most
commercial chocolate, which can exceed 55% of its total content.

Here the difference between commercial chocolate and quality
chocolate is brought sharply into focus: the balance between cocoa
solids and sugar is reversed. Most quality chocolate contains 60%–
70% cocoa solids and 40%–30% sugar; in commercial chocolate the
volume of cocoa solids can drop below 30%.

Commercial chocolate also contains additional vegetable fat.
UK legislation allows up to 5% of such fats, which act as substitutes
for cocoa butter, and it is these fats that are responsible for any
greasy aftertaste in the mouth and a clingy sensation on the palate.

Cocoa content is the key factor – that is to say the combined total of cocoa butter and cocoa solids. The higher this cocoa mass, the higher quality the chocolate.

References to a high level of sugar and vegetable fats should put you on your guard when searching for premium chocolate. So should artificial vanilla flavouring known as vanillin. However, pure vanilla, sometimes referred to as "Vanille Bourbon", is a delicious and time-honoured addition to high quality chocolate. Another ingredient is lecithin, a natural emulsifier which helps stabilize chocolate. This is widely used in premium chocolate and is no cause for concern. It is worth noting that labelling regulations vary around the world.

High cocoa content alone is not an absolute sign of perfection. The quality of the cocoa beans used to make the chocolate is what really counts. This is why several manufacturers specialize in making chocolate purely from one specific cocoa bean.

"I came into this world with a relish for life and its gifts, and chocolate happens to be one of the most tempting that one can possibly imagine."

JEANNE BOURIN, FRENCH WRITER AND CHOCOLATE LOVER

TOTAL
INDUL

Tasting and appreciating chocolate has similarities with tasting wine. Smell, appearance, flavour and aftertaste all play their part in assessing and enjoying fine chocolate, just as they do with evaluating and judging fine wine. The essential difference is that wine enters the mouth as a liquid, whereas chocolate transforms deliciously from a solid into a liquid as soon as it settles on the tongue. This is one of its enduring delights.

Top quality chocolate begins to melt a few seconds after coming into contact with your fingers. This is due to its high level of cocoa butter, which melts at a temperature of 34°C (93.2°F). (Mass-produced commercial chocolate melts at a lower temperature because it contains less cocoa butter.)

Sweetly fragrant in aroma, the smell of the chocolate should not be overpowering. Nor should it be without any smell at all.

A quick look will indicate the condition of the chocolate. It should be an even shade of dark mahogany in colour, free from streaks or "bloom" caused by moisture or heat; free too from air bubbles, cracks or other blemishes.

Fine quality chocolate is silky to the touch and snaps crisply thanks to the crystalline structure of cocoa butter.

Now for the best part. Pop a piece of chocolate on your tongue and wait for the intoxicating results. Good quality chocolate will start to melt immediately, filling your mouth with a blend of flavours, rising from a smooth, creamy base. There should be no hint of wax or grease in the taste: those are signs of added vegetable fats.

Like great wines, great chocolate should have an aftertaste which lingers for several minutes, clean and free from residue, leaving a sensation of satisfaction and peaceful contentment.

GENCE

SWEET SEDUCTION

$$\boxed{\textit{Chocolate and romance}}$$

> *"Candy*
> *Is dandy*
> *But liquor*
> *Is quicker."*

OGDEN NASH, "REFLECTIONS ON ICE-BREAKING"

Chocolate and sex have always been willing bed mates.

Archaeologists have discovered that, centuries ago, chocolate played an important part in the lives of top-flight Mayans, especially at their weddings. Montezuma, the last Aztec emperor, who reigned at the beginning of the 16th century, used to drink 50 cups of chocolate every day to keep him going in the bedroom every night. Casanova, the celebrated 18th-century "adventurer", whose name has become synonymous with amorous intrigues, strongly believed in its power between the sheets; difficult as it may be to comprehend today, a cup of hot chocolate was his favourite bedtime tipple.

Most significantly, from the male standpoint at any rate, chocolate seems to have a special allure for

women. A perfect chocolate soufflé, a mouth-watering selection of sinfully scrumptious continental bonbons, a drum of delicately crafted champagne truffles, even a well-timed nibble from a commercial chocolate bar – the smell, texture and sense of sheer indulgence of chocolate has won the heart (and much more besides) of many a fair lady.

As an aid to seduction, chocolate has science on its side. Among the chemicals it releases in the body is phenylethylamine, that is naturally found in the brain as well, which acts with dopamine, another chemical found in our pleasure centres. Together, these boost blood pressure and heart rate, while heightening sensation. Little wonder that erotic desire and passion are only a bite or two away.

Throughout its history, chocolate has been viewed as a source of illicit temptation. In the spring of 1712, when nature began to stir and early thoughts of love were in the air, this warning appeared in the London magazine, the *Spectator*:

"I shall advise my fair readers to be in particular manner careful how they meddle with romances, chocolates, novels and the like inflamers, which I look upon as very dangerous to be made use of . . ."

This, of course, was written at a time when chocolate was enjoyed solely as a drink. When mass-market eating chocolate began to appear in the middle of the following century a galaxy of further temptations was laid bare.

The exotic aroma of chocolate works its spell on the male of the species too, whether in the form of lip gloss or perfume. There are chocolate "notes" in perfumes like "Angel" by Thierry Mugler and "Rush" by Gucci – irresistible combinations of chocolate and vanilla.

Conditioned by nature to crave sweet, fatty food, the human senses find chocolate almost impossible to ignore. And here lies its delicious dichotomy: sinfully tempting and satisfying, chocolate also brings with it guilt about calories and recollections of secret bingeing. If Adam and Eve were wandering the Garden of Eden today, there would be little contest between the apple and chocolate when it came to selecting the forbidden fruit.

Sensuous, sleek and seductively melting to the touch, chocolate has an erotic potential few other foods can rival. From the first date, when, so advertisers would have us believe, a box of chocolates was once de rigueur for any aspiring suitor, to the unparalleled intimacy

of applying and "removing" chocolate body paint, chocolate has been the hand-maid of seduction and sexual gratification for centuries.

Little wonder, then, that the giving of innumerable boxes filled with the dark, subtle attractions of chocolate truffles, fondants, fudges and creams has become an established part of the mating ritual we celebrate every St Valentine's Day.

*"A gourmet who thinks of calories
is like a tart who looks at her watch."*

JAMES BEARD, AMERICAN FOOD WRITER

If eating chocolate is the sublime fulfilment of expectation, cooking with it is rich in glorious anticipation.

As one of the most versatile and varied foods enjoyed by man, chocolate can range in colour from delicate beige to glossy ebony-brown. In combination with other foods, its texture and taste are almost limitless. Light and succulent in a mousse, deliciously dense and sticky in hot puddings, chocolate can appeal to the sweetest sweet-tooth, lend a tangy bitterness to delicate truffles, or add body to a savoury sauce.

With such a palette of taste treats available, the golden rule is to use the finest chocolate for cooking – the better the chocolate you cook with, the better the gâteau, dessert or sauce you end up with.

You will not go far wrong if you use couverture chocolate. This is a suspension of sugar and cocoa particles in cocoa butter. All the makers of premium chocolate produce couverture chocolate. But do not let the name confuse you. Although "couverture" is the

RECIPES
FOR
PLEASURE

Chocolate and orange mousse.

*A sensational Swiss gâteau crowned with Lindt thins,
produced with the most exquisite chocolate varieties.*

French word for "covering", couverture chocolate is vastly superior to the confectionery products known as "covering" or "coating" chocolate – and it is "couverture" chocolate that you want to use.

Here are a couple of recipes indicating imaginative ways in which chocolate can be used in the kitchen and enjoyed at the table.

CHOCOLATE PASTA

For the pasta

250 g (9 oz) plain flour
100 g (4 oz) cocoa powder
25 g (1 oz) caster sugar
Pinch of cinnamon
4 eggs
½ teaspoon vanilla essence

For the sauce

6 teaspoons good quality, clear honey
6 tablespoons chopped pistachio nuts

Sift the flour with the cocoa powder, and stir in the sugar and cinnamon. Make a well in the centre of the dry ingredients and add the eggs and vanilla essence, and mix to a smooth dough.

Roll out the dough on a floured surface until 3 mm (⅛ in) thick. With a pastry wheel cut the dough into strips 2 cm (¾ in) wide and about 18 cm (7 in) long. (If you have a pasta machine, you can use it to roll and cut the dough).

Cook the pasta in unsalted, boiling water for 3 minutes. Drain and divide between four warmed plates. Drizzle a generous teaspoon of honey and sprinkle pistachio nuts over each serving.

SCANDINAVIAN ICED BERRIES WITH HOT WHITE CHOCOLATE SAUCE

This sensational dessert is a speciality enjoyed by diners at top London restaurants: the Caprice and the Ivy.

It was invented on the recommendation of a customer, who had had something similar in Sweden. The kitchen experimented for ages with the sauce until they came up with the melted white chocolate buttons. This is the simplest and most moreish pudding you will ever make and could become a dinner party classic.

For this recipe you can buy either frozen mixed berries or raspberries. Alternatively, freeze your own selection of berries on a flat tray then put them into a bag in the freezer and use them on a rainy day. Larger berries, such as strawberries and big blackberries, are not recommended for this recipe as they do not defrost quickly enough.

600 g (1¼ lb) good quality white chocolate buttons
600 ml (20 fl oz) double cream
1 kg (2 lb) frozen berries (100–200 g/3–4 oz per person)

Place the chocolate buttons and the cream in a bowl over a pan of simmering water for 20–30 minutes, stirring every so often. When the sauce is hot, we are ready to go.

Five minutes before serving, put the berries on to dessert plates and leave at room temperature to lose a little of their chill. Transfer the chocolate sauce into a serving jug. Place the berries in front of your guests and pour the hot chocolate sauce at the table. Insist that you cover the berries generously for the best result.

It is important to use good quality chocolate for cooking.

HOT CHOCOLATE SOUFFLÉ

125 g (4 oz) bitter or plain chocolate, chopped
150 ml (¼ pint) double cream
3 egg yolks
2 tablespoons Grand Marnier, Cointreau or Curaçao
5 egg whites
Pinch of salt
4 tablespoons caster suger
175 ml (6 fl oz) whipping cream

Pre-heat the oven to 200°C/400°F/gas mark 6. Butter and sugar a 1.25 l (2 pt) soufflé dish. Melt the chocolate and cream together in a heavy-bottomed saucepan over very gentle heat. Remove from the heat and beat in the egg yolks, one at a time. Stir in the liqueur.

Whisk the egg whites and salt together until stiff. Add the sugar and continue to whisk until the mixture turns glossy. Fold a few tablespoons of the whites into the chocolate mixture to lighten it. Add this mixture to the remaining whites and fold together carefully. Spoon the mixture into the prepared dish and bake for 12–14 minutes. Lightly whip the cream and serve separately.

COOL,

<blockquote>
"Chocolate is something you have an affair with."
GENEEN ROTH, *FEEDING THE HUNGRY HEART*
</blockquote>

DARK

Chocolate ice cream

As long ago as the middle of the 17th century, a form of chocolate ice cream was being enjoyed in the Italian city of Naples. At that time Naples was under Spanish control and chocolate from Spanish colonies in the Caribbean and South America was hugely popular in the city.

Italian ice cream continues to be among the very best in the world, but delicious ice creams can be made at home, as the following recipes show.

(opposite)
Ice cream with delicate wafers of premium chocolate – a taste treat to complete any meal.

STIBLE

CHOCOLATE ICE CREAM

    4 egg yolks
    50 g (2 oz) raw cane sugar
    275 ml (½ pt) milk
    175 g (6 oz) plain chocolate
    275 ml (½ pt) cream

Beat the egg yolks with the sugar in a medium-sized mixing bowl.
Bring the milk nearly to the boil and pour over the egg yolks, stirring
all the time until cool. Set aside. Break the chocolate into a bowl and
heat over a pan of simmering water, stirring gently until melted. Now
return the egg yolk mixture, sugar and milk to the saucepan over a
low heat and stir all the time until it coats the back of the spoon.
Take it off the heat. Add the chocolate to the egg mixture. Mix well
and set aside to cool. Whip the cream and fold into the mixture, chill
and freeze.

CHOCOLATE TRUFFLE ICE CREAM

    4 egg yolks
    50 g (2 oz) raw cane sugar
    275 ml (½ pt) milk
    75 g (3 oz) plain chocolate
    75 g (3 oz) ground hazelnuts
    275 ml (½ pt) cream

Beat the egg yolks with the sugar in a medium-sized mixing bowl until
thick. Scald the milk and pour over the egg yolks, stirring all the time.
Set aside while you break the chocolate into a bowl and heat over a pan
of simmering water, stirring gently until melted. Now return the egg
yolks, sugar and milk to the saucepan and stir over a low heat until it
coats the back of the spoon. Remove from the heat and continue stirring
for a few moments. Beat the chocolate into the egg mixture. Add the
ground hazelnuts. Set aside to cool. Whip the cream and fold into the
mixture. Chill and freeze.

CUP

ID'S NIGHTCAP

(*Drinking chocolate*)

*"Coffee from the top of the cup,
chocolate from the bottom."*
VENETIAN PROVERB

The great popularity of drinking chocolate, which swept through Europe following its arrival in the 17th century, was memorably recorded by a number of notable figures. Casanova, who found it so invigorating at bedtime, is said to have preferred drinking chocolate to champagne.

Mozart placed it centre-stage in a scene in his opera *Cosi Fan Tutte*, in which the lady's maid, Despina, complains of the time she spends preparing drinking chocolate for her mistress, tormented by the delicious smell without ever tasting it. That is until her will power gives way and she allows herself a secret sip and discovers why drinking hot chocolate has been a source of comfort, secret pleasure and pure indulgence for the best part of 350 years.

In the 17th century, Queen Maria Theresa elevated the drinking of chocolate to such a status at the court of Louis XIV of France, that a new industry developed producing cups and pots for chocolate drinkers. By the end of the century wine merchants in France were

grumbling that the popularity of chocolate was
threatening their livelihoods.

During the late 17th and 18th centuries
chocolate houses were important meeting places
for gentlemen of influence. This was particularly true
in London, where the habit of drinking chocolate
spread rapidly during the reign of Charles II, in the
second half of the 17th century.

Chocolate was a popular breakfast drink until the
middle of the 18th century, after which it began to
give way to tea and coffee. By then the heyday of
chocolate houses had passed. Many either closed
down or changed the nature of their business.

White's, the celebrated gentlemen's club in London,
opened in 1693 as White's Chocolate House,
before becoming a famous gambling house and later
transforming into the oldest and grandest of the
St James's gentlemen's clubs.

The drinking chocolate which first took Europe
by storm was a very different beverage from the
warm, comforting, milky drinking chocolate enjoyed
today. Claret, egg yolks, Port and Madeira, as well
as hot water, were all mixed with grated chocolate
powder to produce drinks enriched with spices.

In England, Sir Hans Sloane, whose long life
spanned the second half of the 17th century
and the first half of the 18th, was the first to
popularize hot chocolate made with milk.
As a celebrated physician, he promoted his
chocolate and milk drink as a medical potion,
after observing the effect cocoa had on
reviving sickly infants in Jamaica.

Sir Hans Sloane's delicious recipe remained a closely-guarded secret, which earned him a considerable fortune before he sold it to a chocolate manufacturer. The rights to his potion were eventually bought by the Cadbury Brothers in 1849, who named their new chocolate drink Sir Hans Sloane's Milk Chocolate, after its original inventor.

By the time the Cadburys acquired Sir Hans' recipe, chocolate was becoming more readily available. Until the 19th century, it had remained the preserve of the well-to-do – a drink on a par with champagne today.

Although coffee and tea supplanted chocolate at the breakfast table, drinking chocolate has always remained a popular, warming beverage, especially at bedtime – and not always as a means of quickly falling asleep, as we have already seen.

For a truly memorable bedtime treat, allow yourself a taste of real, unashamed luxury, such as this, from Britain's acclaimed Chocolate Society:

THE CHOCOLATE SOCIETY'S HOT CHOCOLATE

The flakes of chocolate produced by The Chocolate Society for making hot chocolate are made by grating some of the finest couverture chocolate you can buy.

~ Put 5 g (1 tsp) of chocolate per person in a bowl.
~ Bring to the boil 10 fl oz (½ pint) of full-cream milk per person.
~ Add ¼ milk to chocolate and stir until dissolved.
~ Add rest of milk and whip.
~ Add sugar to taste.
~ Serve in a small coffee cup accompanied by a bowl of chilled whipped cream for added indulgence.

THE
TASTE
OF
PERFECTION

> Leading chocolatiers

"Venice is like eating an entire box of chocolate liqueurs in one go."

TRUMAN CAPOTE, AMERICAN AUTHOR

From Venice to Venice Beach, from Paris to Park Avenue, the world's finest chocolates can be found right around the globe, wherever quality and a taste for the best in life is valued and enjoyed.

While Europe remains the principal destination for chocolate aficionados, examples of the best chocolate from the best chocolate makers can be tracked down in most of the world's great cities.

Here is a selection of names to tempt you.

CHARBONNEL ET WALKER

A mixture of French and English by name and with a thriving export trade to the USA, Charbonnel et Walker has been established among Britain's foremost chocolatiers since 1875. In that year the Prince of Wales (later King Edward VII) encouraged Mme Charbonnel to come to London from the Parisian chocolate house of Maison Boissier, to join forces with Mrs Walker in forming a chocolatiers' and confectionery house in London's fashionable Bond Street where it can still be found today.

Many of the company's recipes are from Mme Charbonnel's original recipe book. All its chocolates are hand-made in Tunbridge Wells and until the 1950s each chocolate was stamped with a number to help identify it on the menu included with the selection.

Charbonnel et Walker, gracing London's Bond Street.

CHOCOLATES EL REY

When the family-owned business of Tuozzo Zozaya & Cia was established in the Venezuelan capital, Caracas, in 1929 they named the chocolate they began producing, El Rey – The King.

The tradition of making exceptional chocolate, on which the company was founded, is as strong today as it was 70 years ago. Although El Rey is equipped with machinery to match any in Europe, it is the quality of the cocoa beans it uses which defines and maintains its enduring standard.

Only Venezuelan cocoa beans are used to make El Rey chocolate. Grown on small plantations, as they have been for centuries, these are nurtured and prepared with the utmost care. The proof is in the eating.

THE CHOCOLATE SOCIETY

Formed in 1990 by three committed chocolate enthusiasts, The Chocolate Society has established itself within a decade as the British champion for the use and enjoyment of true chocolate, for both the confectioner and the chocolate lover.

The Chocolate Society produces an extensive range of mouth-watering, hand-made truffles and chocolates. These are available by mail order, or from the Society's shop in London's exclusive Belgravia. It also sells chocolate made by Valrhona, the French producer of one of the world's most outstanding couvertures.

GODIVA

Today Godiva chocolates, for many the benchmark of excellence in Belgian chocolate making, are enjoyed by consumers throughout the world. In the USA, Godiva continues to be the leader in premium chocolate, with over 200 speciality boutiques in major US cities and over 1,000 additional outlets in fine department and speciality stores.

The company was founded by the Draps family in the Belgian capital, Brussels, in 1926. Joseph Draps named his chocolate company after Lady Godiva, the 11th-century wife of a Danish ruler in central England. It was Lady Godiva who undertook to ride unclothed through the streets of Coventry in order to spare its citizens further heavy taxes imposed by her husband. Her honour and sense of duty became a fitting symbol for the Godiva company which has been perfecting the concept of premium chocolate for over 70 years.

The company still follows recipes created by Joseph Draps, who established Godiva's innovative selection of elegant, European shell-moulded designs and beautiful packaging, which underscore the company's reputation for design excellence.

LINDT & SPRÜNGLI

Lindt & Sprüngli has been producing fine quality chocolates since 1845. Based in Kilchberg, just outside Zurich, Lindt & Sprüngli makes a wide range of high quality chocolates which are exported worldwide. The quality of its recipes and presentation has earned Lindt & Sprüngli its reputation as one of the finest chocolate makers in the world.

Lindt's Swiss Tradition inlaid assorted pralines make the perfect gift for any occasion. Choose from: Swiss Tradition Milk, containing a delicious selection of milk pralines; Mixed, which contains a medley of exquisite milk, plain and white chocolates with unique and irresistible fillings; and de Luxe, the ultimate box of chocolates containing an array of finest white, milk, plain and liqueur chocolates.

Other mouth-watering products to look out for from Lindt are the soft, melting twist-wrapped Lindor truffles and the range of Excellence chocolate bars in a variety of flavours including Natural Vanilla white chocolate, Extra Creamy Milk and 70% Cocoa Dark.

SCHARFFEN BERGER CHOCOLATE MAKER

As the only American chocolate company founded in the last 50 years, California-based Scharffen Berger is not afraid to hark back to time-honoured traditions and principles in its quest "to make the richest, most flavourful chocolate from the purest and best cacao [cocoa beans] that can be found".

Time consuming and arduous as the process is, Scharffen Berger has turned back the clock when it comes to making chocolate. Using restored vintage machinery imported from Europe, the company specializes in producing superb quality chocolate from carefully selected beans grown near the equator. These include rare Venezuelan criollos, as well as beans from Madagascar, Trinidad, Ghana and Papua New Guinea.

Large crystal cane sugar and whole bean Tahitian and Bourbon vanillas are mixed and ground with selected batches of beans, before being conched into a lush liquid chocolate.

Like all top quality couvertures, Scharffen Berger is as sought after by leading chefs throughout North America, as it is by connoisseurs of true chocolate. That is no small achievement for a company that was only founded in 1996.

VALRHONA

Long acknowledged to be "Le Chocolat de Grands Chefs", chocolate from the French house of Valrhona is of the finest quality. Three-quarters of the company's sales are to professional clients who value the consistent quality of Valrhona's output.

Valrhona seeks out the best cocoa at source. In the course of a couple of years, Valrhona's buyer reviews an average of 80 cocoa plantations, in 22 countries, rigorously examining their harvesting and production methods to ensure a consistent crop from pod to production line.

The result of this dedicated attention to quality is Valrhona's unsurpassed reputation as a maker of grands crus chocolates. These include Manjari, a delicious dark chocolate of 64% cocoa solids with a hint of red berries and Jivara, a creamy milk chocolate enriched with malt and brown sugar, with a high cocoa content of 40%.

A chocolate tour

For many aficionados, Paris is the chocolate capital of the world, which makes it a fitting point of departure for a tour of some of the leading chocolate shops on both sides of the Atlantic.

On the Place de la Madeleine, one of three premises belonging to Fauchon, the grandest and most famous food "shop" in Paris, is given over to chocolate. Chocolate cakes and pastries as well as a huge range of chocolates themselves make a visit to Fauchon imperative for any serious chocolate enthusiast.

After starting out in business on the rue du Bac nearly 30 years ago, the French chocolate guru Christian Constant now operates from a delightful shop on the rue d'Assas. An expert on cocoa growing, he is a master of exciting and exotic flavours which read more like a perfumer's catalogue than a chocolatier's.

In a city graced by many of the world's leading makers of chocolate, Robert Linxe, founder of La Maison du Chocolat, is recognized as its premier pioneering chocolatier. Starting in business in Paris in 1965, his was the only shop in the city making fine hand-made chocolate confections every day, to ensure their freshness. At his shop in the rue du Faubourg Saint-Honoré (one of five he now has in Paris) he became the first person to set up a business devoted entirely to chocolate.

Twenty years ago Robert Linxe began his celebrated partnership with Valrhona, whose couverture he has helped to establish as a world leader. Traditional in appearance, La Maison du Chocolat is a temple to the best of the chocolatier's art. But this is a tradition built on a solid business foundation; Robert Linxe's chocolate "laboratory" in Colombes produces 14 tons of chocolates for the Christmas market alone.

Alongside the specialist chocolatiers already mentioned (Charbonnel et Walker and The Chocolate Society) London has

Style, flair and superlative chocolate distinguish chocolates from Rococo.

others with an equally distinctive identity and a staunch commitment to excellence and quality.

A little over a mile up the King's Road from Sloane Square brings the chocolate disciple to the door of Rococo where, since 1983, some of the world's finest chocolates have been offered for sale against a background of constantly changing colours and shapes, that reflect the art school training of its founder and inspiration, Chantal Coady. Rococo specializes in hand-made bars of exquisite chocolate, made exclusively for the shop from the world's finest cocoa beans.

Outside Prestat.

Prestat, which lies in the Princes Arcade in Piccadilly, is chocolatier to Queen Elizabeth II and includes velvety, cocoa-dusted fresh-cream Napoleon II truffles among its exclusive tantalizing temptations. These are made to a 19th-century recipe known only to Prestat and take their name from the Emperor Napoleon III, who lived in exile in King Street, in St James's, only a truffle-throw from Prestat's exotically appointed shop.

A short step from Prestat brings you to Fortnum & Mason, London's premier food emporium which was still importing its own cocoa beans in the late 1920s, to make the 50 different chocolates listed in its catalogue at the time. Seventy years on most of these are still available, although production has long since moved from Fortnum's Piccadilly address. At Fortnum's you can buy chocolates from around the chocolate-making world.

For the largest selection of chocolate in London (and in the whole of the UK as well) you should travel to Harrods. In addition to its own truffles, which are hand-made on the shop floor, the world famous Knightsbridge shop sells chocolates from Belgium, England, France and Switzerland.

Switzerland has long been renowned for the superb quality of its chocolate and throughout the country dedicated chocolatiers maintain that tradition today. In Geneva, Chocolats Rohr, with shops at 3 place du Molard and 42 rue du Rhône, are famous for their pralines and assorted chocolates.

Chocolate lovers visiting Zurich will never be far from one of the shops owned by Confiserie Sprüngli, which has 12 outlets in the city (including two at the airport). Chocolates from Sprüngli are still carefully made by hand according to traditional methods first used when the company was founded by David Sprüngli in Zurich's Marktgasse in 1836.

Belgian chocolate is as popular around the world as Swiss chocolate, with brands like Godiva and Leonidas spearheading its

Fortnum & Mason's Coffee and Cream selection includes succulent truffles and moreish coffee beans.

international success through conventional retail sites as well as the growing trade in confectionery sales on-line. Godiva can be visited at its flagship shop at 1000 Grande Place in Brussels. Leonidas has more than 1,750 outlets around the world selling its celebrated pralines, of which there are now over 80 different varieties. The original Leonidas shop in Brussels was opened in a single rented room on the boulevard Anspach which is still a Mecca for globetrotting chocolatiers.

At first glance many of New York's leading chocolate speciality stores have a comforting familiarity: Godiva arrived in America in 1966 and with over 200 speciality boutiques in major US cities and over 1,000 additional outlets in fine department and speciality stores, it has established itself as the leader in premium chocolates.

Leonidas has its New York headquarters on Madison Avenue at number 485. One block south of Wall Street, at 3 Hanover Square, you will find Leonidas' European style espresso bar featuring Illy Espresso and Cappuccino coffees as well as a tempting selection of Leonidas pralines. These are also available at Chelsea Market Baskets, purveyors of distinctive gourmet food at 75 Ninth Avenue.

However, many of New York's serious chocolate enthusiasts flock to La Maison du Chocolat at 1018 Madison Avenue, where they treat themselves to what is widely regarded as the best Parisian chocolate in the city.

On the west coast, Scharffen Berger in Berkeley, California, is setting similarly high standards for quality US chocolates. Close by, the Ghirardelli Chocolate Company has been making chocolate in and around San Francisco since 1852.

Five centuries after Europeans first encountered chocolate in the New World, the beans which the peoples of Central America once prepared as an offering to please their gods are now used to make one of the most moreish and delicious culinary creations enjoyed by people the world over.

GLOSSARY

CACAO Name given to harvested cocoa beans before processing.

CHOCOLATE PASTE Pure chocolate block with no added sugar.

COCOA BEAN Seed of the cocoa tree found in the cocoa pod.

COCOA BUTTER Natural oil of the cocoa bean.

COCOA LIQUOR Another term for cocoa mass.

COCOA MASS Liquid paste formed from grinding cocoa beans.

COCOA POD Fruit of the cocoa tree, containing cocoa beans.

CONCHING Production process in which chocolate is smoothed and refined.

COUVERTURE Blend of cocoa particles and sugar in cocoa butter; fine quality chocolate.

CRIOLLO Rare cocoa bean producing chocolate of exceptional character.

FERMENTATION Production process to reduce acidity and develop aroma in cocoa beans.

FORASTERO Cocoa bean producing everyday chocolate; 85% of world's total production.

GANACHE Blend of chocolate and cream (and sometimes butter) in truffles.

LECITHIN Natural emulsifier used to stabilize chocolate.

NIBS Cocoa beans broken into particles and removed from their shells.

TEMPERING Delicate process of amalgamating and setting chocolate.

TRINITARIO Hybrid cocoa bean making fine chocolate.

TRUFFLE Confection made from ganache and couverture and dusted in cocoa powder.

VANILLIN Artificial vanilla flavouring.

VEGETABLE FATS Substitute fats and oils used in place of pure cocoa butter.

XOCOLATL Pre-Columbian drink made from ground cocoa beans.